forever in two seconds

Sanika Mohile

BookLeaf Publishing

Presentation by *BookLeaf Publishing*

Web: www.bookleafpub.com

E-mail: info@bookleafpub.com

ISBN: 9789357617208

First edition 2022

The Spill

Tell me your favourite colour,
I'll find every shade of it,
I'll mix them on the canvas by hand
And paint every woven thread,
Each hue reminding me of you and the colour
you brought to my life,

Make me yours, not just in this moment
But every, living, breathing second of everyday,
my soul will burn for you

the thought of forever,
was never mine to hold,
but living without you makes me not want to
imagine...

After moments in time created and shared,
synced heartbeats
I'll never forget how it feels,
to be enlaced with you...

But now,
All that's left...
Is a spill on the canvas
Forever tainted on my heart...

The one

No matter what version of him I am facing,
Each and every single type is worth risking and
taking,

For a split second,
My heart lingered with hope,
Maybe there's a chance,
To change the present,

I look away and the light begins to dim,
maybe i'm clinging onto an expired version of
him.
But how,
How do i forget?
For death comes upon humans,
and never memories...

Incomplete

I've been wishing on shooting stars,
Of all i wish i could say,
But the words that have been rotting in my
stomach,
slowly claw their way up,
And suddenly i'm choking and drowning on the
words I did not say,
The feelings i kept away...

We set our souls ablaze in an everlasting heat,
If the love in this world is a continuous feeling
of incomplete,
then who am i to compete?

But of course, all broken things can be put
together,
If only, my heart wasn't a feather
So now I bid you farewell,
And hope my heart unswells

I leave my incomplete heart in your care,
And only hope one day you may complete it,
With one more worthy than me

Roses

When you prick a rose,
You don't pay heed to its thorns,
To its painful and unattractive flaws
To its withering life,
Instead, you stand in awe of the main attraction,
The petals…

But even roses understand,
That beauty is makeshift
And so it lifts the thorns that protect its stem,
Protecting its only source of life

To my parents,

Parents, they truly are the world's most selfless
people,
They'll pull the moon down for you,
To brighten the darkest nights
They'll rearrange the stars in the sky,
Just to see you smile

They'll give you the sun
So it can shine on your cloudy days
They'll pour down rain on the driest days,
When you need some water to rest
They'll call a storm,
When they realise you're hurt

They'll give you the world, to show how much
they care
They'll give you everything they can,
The sun, the stars, the moon
Everything. Just for you.
They truly are selfless beyond all.

For you

If you really think about it you have no idea
what you look like.
You see yourself in the mirror,
the pictures,
the videos,
the albums,
Sure, people may tell you what you look like

But still, do you really know?
Do you know what a stranger thinks of you,
as you run behind the bus with your brown hair
swaying behind you in the wind,
Your eyes like the colour of the earth, sun kissed
in the morning light as you anxiously wait for
the next one?

Have you seen the way your smile beams from
its edges everytime you talk about something
you love?
Have you seen the way your eyes light up in awe
at the moon and the sky?

You may think you know what you look like,
But in reality,
You've got absolutely. no. idea.

So why do you refuse,
Refuse to see the beauty you illuminate from
within?
The way your elegance radiates throughout your
whole body,
Through your soul,
your mind,
your heart
Even, as you walk and smile

So just be enough for yourself
Show up for yourself
The rest of the world can wait...

Growth

There are people that love taking pictures of the
moons,
Though it's the same each time,

People that love taking pictures of the sunsets,
Though it's the same sun setting,

But each and every time,
It's still beautifully unique in its own way.

Now think of yourself as the moon and the sun,
Everyday you wake up feeling as the same
person,
But every year,
Every month,
Every week,
Every day,
Every hour,
Every minute,
Every second,
You are forever growing, changing and evolving

So don't you ever once doubt for even a second
in your growth and how far YOU'VE come as a
person.

Almost, but not quite

I once read a poem,
About how the sun and the moon were lovers
The sun would set
And the moon would rise
There was only one time in space,
Where they would see each other face to face
Oh how they longed for each other but could
never be

But no one talks about the stars or the clouds
And how their love was so loud and proud
Almost there,
But never quite there
So if the love in this world is never quite
complete
Then maybe this world is full of deceit

You and I

I have late night conversations with the waves
like a giant fist, they rise up and slam into the
shore, savage and angry
Only to pull away snatching pieces of the sand's
soul away each time,
Like a broken record on repeat,
Longing for more and more,
My brain has you memorised,
I'd recognise you blind even with freedom in
sight.
I should've realised that you were hell in
disguise.

And maybe you did love me, who knows
But words are words and actions are actions
And your actions cut deeper than a knife
Maybe you did care, maybe i was your
favourite, as you claim
Or maybe, just maybe
I was a puzzle left for you to solve,
Putting me together piece by piece, only to break
me again in the end

The bitterness, the emptiness and the endless
void that leads to nowhere.

I've cried enough tears to fill an entire ocean
To a point where even the ocean took pity on me
You introduced me to a vibe you couldn't
maintain,
When consistency and communication is all i
wanted,
You showed me the wrath of the waves during
the storm

For you Pt 2

With a face carved by Da Vinci himself,
Her brown eyes shone like the finest stars on a
dark night,
The universe made her from the strongest roots
of a tree,
the beauty of the moon,
the storm of an ocean
the glowing embers of a sunset
and most importantly,
With the blessings of an angel up above.

Beauty of life

I will never understand those who can't see the
beauty in life,
Acting as if it's something to search for,
Rather than to indulge in.

How do they not see,
The way the trees branch out into a beautiful
maze of leaves,
Each one reaching for the stars,
The way the white dandelions dance in the air to
the symphony of the wind,
The way the birds hum their lullabies,
The way the soft clouds create a masterpiece in
the bright skies
The way the wind whisper and dance with the
leaves
The way the colours of the sky twirl with each
other…
Each and every single day

They've gotten so used to seeing this every day,
That they simply don't appreciate the little
things
The things,
That a child stands in awe of…

A child doesn't need to search,
To see,
To find…

They can see what's in front of them,
All the time.

The inner ocean

The ocean sat still and calm, reflecting the sky
like a mirror.
"How i wish i was as beautiful as the ocean" she
sighed

What she couldn't see was how,
The ocean aspired to be as alluring as her,
And how when it stormed,
The ocean was shedding all its flaws,
Just to resemble her cries
Yet she danced in its tears so gracefully
The droplets of rain calmly nestling in her hair

She failed to see how
The water was merely a measly attempt from the
ocean,
To capture her beauty in its purest and most
rarest form

A symphony in autumn

Everything looks like a haze at this hour,
In the hour before the sun has a chance to ascend
into the sky.

The fog rises like coffee steam through the
buildings,
And we watch the world,
Shake bark off her bones unheard,
Everything falling and painted shades of
marigold

If you don't believe in magic,
You must never have gone driving in the season
of
Autumn,
And that's fairly tragic.

Simplistic

She was in love with books,
The kind that hook,
Enjoyed her own company,
But also liked being accompanied

She was satisfied,
Neither dumb nor smart,
happy nor sad
loud nor quiet

She breezed through the the day as the wind
pushed her
She was just existing
She thought that was constricting,

And this,
This, was her greatest strength,
Yet also her most destructive weakness.

The moon and I

I reach out to touch the moon,
I can feel the glint of light on broken glass,
I can taste the moonlight that rains upon me
I can hear the sounds of the crickets chirping a
melodious hum,

I look up and realise there are billions of people
under the same moon,
How do we fail to see,
That we are all connected by nature,
by the shimmering silvery light that consumes us
and our feelings each night.
We look up to the sky searching for the
luminescent glow
To reassure ourselves that we are in fact, not just
thriving
But living.

Shooting stars

I don't believe in shooting stars,
Or the strums of guitars,
Fallen eyelashes,
Recurring numbers,
Blowing out birthday candles,
Wishing on dandelions.

I don't believe in them,
Yet i can't seem to help myself from wishing
Wishing on all of them anyways,
It's addiction,
Wishing, wanting, begging, praying,
It's greed.

Every wish I make, Every sound i make,
Every step i take, ,
React 3 times to claim,
"If you're seeing this it's meant for you",
Dropping coins in a well,
Looking for 4 leaf clovers,

I don't believe in shooting stars and maybe that's
the issue
I need to believe it, to receive it.
Or maybe, just maybe
All the shooting stars were just mars.

A glimpse into forever

If you ever undermine your worth, think about,
How even the dirt under your feet,
Has outlived you by a millennia
How the trees can know your presence,
Can feel and love you
How the sun turns towards you every morning,
To awake you

Like sunset,
Sunrise,
Moon,
And all the stars between

You can never be lonely.
How could you be when nature itself speaks to
you,
When the moon listens
And the sun glistens
The flowers sway
While the waves wash away

You are worth everything and more.

forever = danger

Forever is immeasurable
Forever isn't years or generations or lifetimes
So be careful when you say forever